Focus

The focus of this book is:

- to use an index,
- to find information from text and photographs.

Tuning In

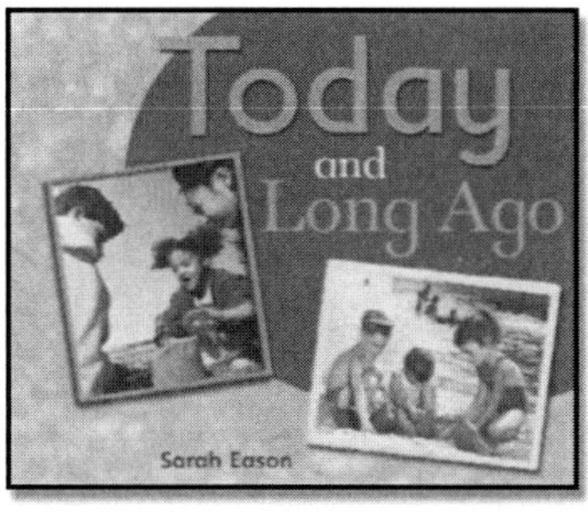

The front cover

Let's read the title together.

Speaking and Listening

What do you expect you are going to read about in this book?

The back cover

Let's read the blurb on the back cover to see what the book is about.

Speaking and Listening

Is it what we expected?

Contents

Let's look at the contents. What are we going to be reading about on page 2?

What are we going to be reading about on page 12?

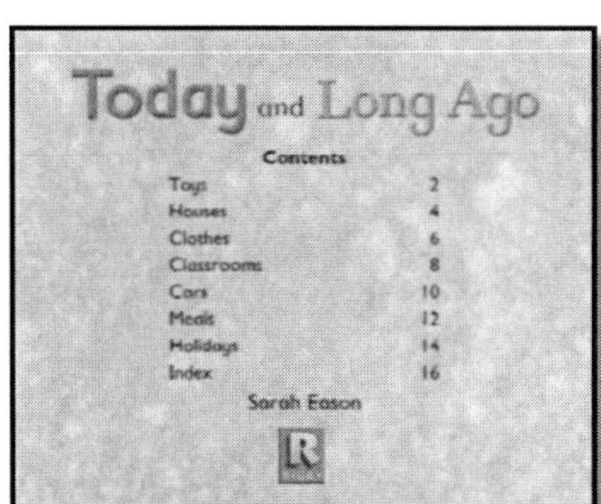

Tuning In

Look at the picture on page 2.

What is it?

Observe and Prompt

Word Recognition

- Check the children can read 'toy' and 'toys' using their decoding skills. Help them with the 'oy' sound if they struggle.

- If the children have difficulty with the word 'today', ask them to break the word down into two syllables – 'to' and 'day', before blending the whole word together.

Tuning In

What is this on page 3?

Which is the toy from long ago? Which would
you like to play with?

Observe and Prompt

Language Comprehension

- Check the children are reading as fluently as possible.
- Ask the children what is the same about the toys.
- Can the children think of any other toys today that children also had long ago?

Tuning In

What is the heading for these two pages?

What kind of house is on page 4?

 Observe and Prompt

Word Recognition

- Check the children can read the words 'house' and 'houses' using their decoding skills.
- Check the children can read 'These' using their decoding skills.
- Check the children can read 'from', 'long' and 'ago' using their decoding skills.

 **Tuning In**

What kind of house is on page 5?

 **Observe and Prompt**

Language Comprehension

- Check the children are reading with appropriate phrasing and are observing punctuation.
- Ask the children how the houses from long ago are different to the houses of today.
- Ask the children what kind of house they live in.

 **Tuning In**

What do you think we are going to look at on these pages?

 **Observe and Prompt**

Word Recognition

- Check the children can read 'clothes' using their decoding skills. Help them with the long 'o' sound (from 'o' and silent 'e') if they struggle.

- Check the children can read 'How' using their decoding skills. Help them with the 'ow' vowel sound if they struggle.

- If the children have difficulty reading 'different', model the blending of this word for them.

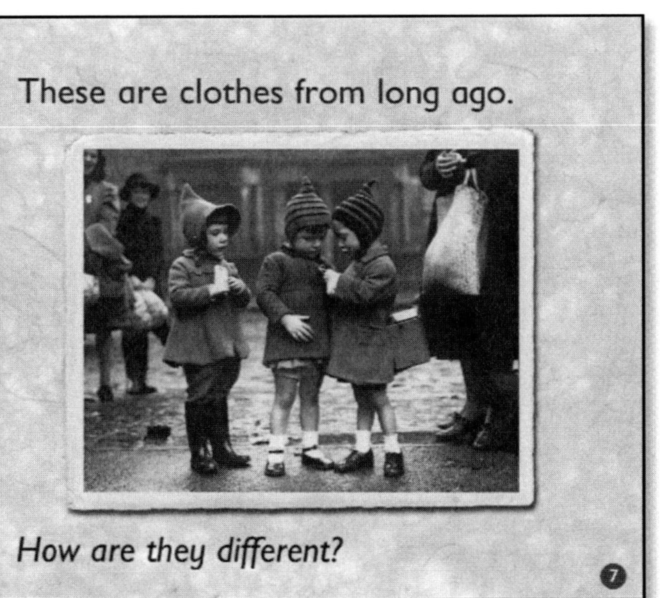

👁 Observe and Prompt

Language Comprehension

- Ask the children which of the pictures show clothes from long ago.
- Ask the children how the clothes from long ago look different to those of today.
- Which clothes do the children prefer? Why?

 **Tuning In**

What do you think we are going to compare on these pages?

Classrooms

This is a classroom today.

8

 **Observe and Prompt**

Word Recognition

- If the children have difficulty with the word 'classroom', ask the children to break the word down into two syllables, before blending the whole word together.

- Check the children can read the sight words 'is', 'your' and 'like'.

- Check the children can read 'ago' using their decoding skills.

 **Observe and Prompt**

Language Comprehension

- Check that the children are reading with phrasing and are observing punctuation.
- Ask the children what the heading is for these pages.
- Ask the children to find two things that are different between these two classrooms, and one thing that is the same.

 **Tuning In**

What are we going to compare on this page?

Speaking and Listening

Which car would you like to ride in?

Observe and Prompt

Word Recognition

- Check the children can read 'car' and 'cars' using their decoding skills.
- Check the children can read the word 'Which' using their decoding skills.
- Can the children read 'best', blending the adjacent consonants at the end of this word?

 **Observe and Prompt**

Language Comprehension

- Check the children are using the punctuation.
- Ask the children which car they like best. Why?

 **Tuning In**

Look at the pictures of the food.

Speaking and Listening

What's your favourite meal?

Meals

This is a meal today.
12

Observe and Prompt

Word Recognition

- Check the children can read 'meal' and 'Meals' using their decoding skills. Help them with the 'ea' sound if they have difficulty.

- If the children have difficulty reading the word 'favourite', model the blending of this word for them.

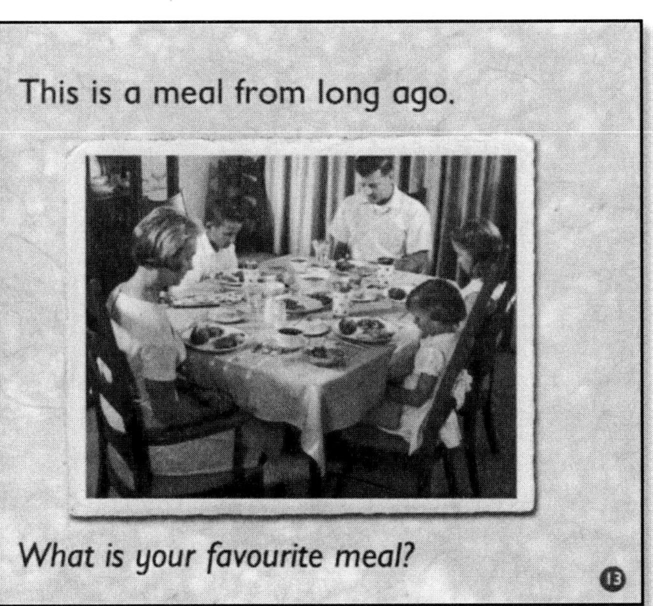

Observe and Prompt

Language Comprehension

- Ask the children what the heading is for these pages.
- Ask the children how the two meals are similar.
- Do the children think the food we eat is different from long ago?

Tuning In

Where are the children?

What are the children doing in the pictures?

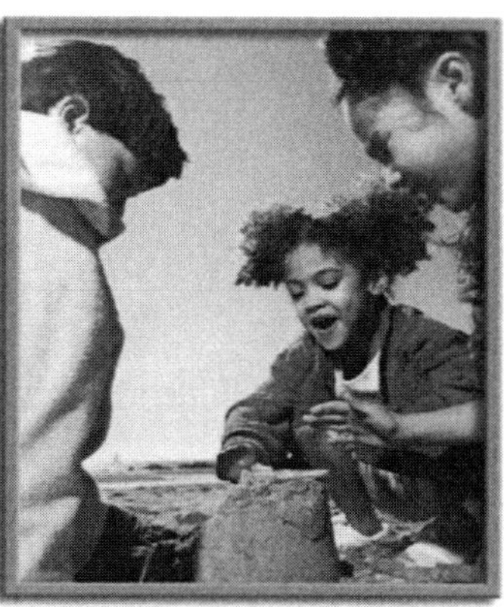

Observe and Prompt

Word Recognition

- If the children have difficulty reading 'holiday', ask them to break it down into three syllables – 'hol', 'i' and 'day', before blending the whole word together from left to right.

- Prompt the children to break down the word 'seaside' into two syllables, before blending the whole word together. Help them with the 'ea' vowel sound if they have difficulty.

- If the children have difficulty with the words 'making' and 'sandcastle', model the blending of these words for them.

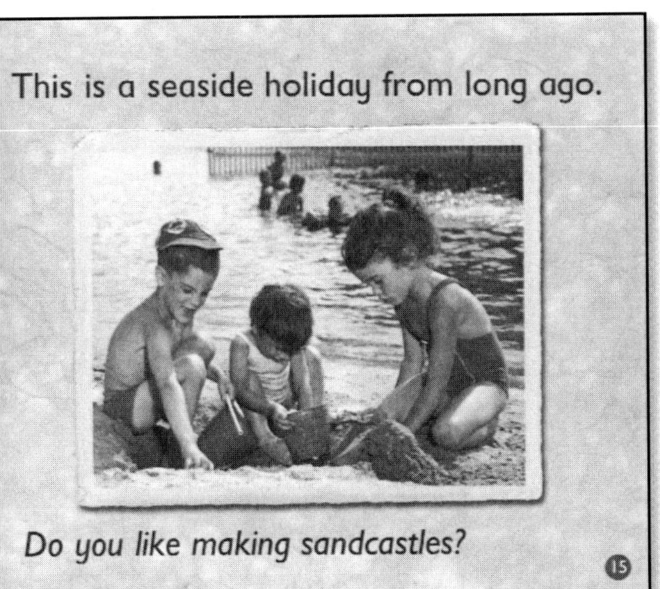

Observe and Prompt

Language Comprehension

- Ask the children what the children in these pictures are doing.
- Do the children think the pictures are similar? In what way?
- Ask the children if they like to build sandcastles at the seaside.

Tuning In

On this page there is a list of words. It is called an index.

Index

cars 10-11

classrooms 8-9

clothes 6-7

holidays 14-15

houses 4-5

meals 12-13

toys 2-3

16

Observe and Prompt

Language Comprehension

- Check the children understand the purpose of the index and can use it effectively.
- Ask the children to use the index to find information about 'holidays'. Ask the children to check these pages.